To request permissions, contact the publisher at bczpublishers@gmail.com

Paperback: ISBN 978-1-7367153-7-6

First Paperback Edition: April 2022

Written by: Mina Soliman
Illustrated by: Cynthia Zeilenga

BCZ Publishers
3365 E Miraloma Ave Ste 205, Anaheim, CA 92806

BCZ
PUBLISHERS

how i helped...

David defeat Goliath

"All those gathered here will know that it is not by sword or spear that the Lord saves"
1 Samuel 17:47

In the center of a peaceful village
I stood mighty and tall
No matter how hard the villagers tried
It was impossible to move this great wall

So I continued to stand arrogant and proud
And day after day cast my shadow on all
The people tried to live the best they could
But I made everything seem so small

Thinking I could never be brought down
I kept hold of the village with a tight grip
Until one day a soft rain began to fall
It started with a gentle drip drip drip

The drizzling rain turned into a vicious storm
As the villagers ran to seek cover
With nowhere to hide, I was left all alone
My shape, I would never recover

It rained for years, and when it stopped
All that was left of this great rock wall
Was a very tiny pebble
So meek and so small

I watched as the villagers rejoiced
They basked in the sun and were so cheerful
Enjoying the budding flowers and flowing streams
And for a short time, no one was fearful

Until... an army led by a giant man
Invaded the village and its people
Goliath threatened their homes and their lives
Bringing with him a great deal of evil

I trembled as I watched the villagers suffer
I wished I was big and mighty like before
But just as I began to lose all hope
A young boy named David slowly reached down to the floor

David and I were both small and humble
Yet he bravely placed me into his sling
Aiming it right at Goliath and his angry snare
With God by our side, David let out one powerful fling

And with that fling, Goliath was defeated
David and I had won
All the glory was given to God
And for that day, my purpose was done

The End.

PUBLISHERS

www.ingramcontent.com/pod-product-compliance
Lightning Source LLC
Chambersburg PA
CBHW042109040426

42448CB00002B/202